concrete pastures
of the beautiful bronx

w r rodriguez

zeugpress

Poems from this book previously appeared in: *The Critic; Dusty Dog; "I didn't know there were Latinos in Wisconsin" Volume II; North Coast Review; The Party Train: A Collection of North American Prose Poetry; Poets on the Line; Turnstile; Two Worlds Walking: Short Stories, Essays, & Poetry by Writers with Mixed Heritages;* and *Welcome to Your Life: Writings for the Heart of Young America.*

Selections from "roosevelt's bust," "logic," and "saint mary's park" appeared in: *Bronx Accent: A Literary and Pictorial History of the Borough,* Lloyd Ultan and Barbara Unger (Rutgers University Press: 2000).

Also by w r rodriguez: *the shoe shine parlor poems et al* (Ghost Pony Press: 1984).

© 2008 w r rodriguez
All rights reserved

ISBN: 978-0-9632201-2-7

Printed in the United States of America
First Edition

Zeugpress

Contents

I
the bootblack 7
my little red fire engine 8
sledgehammer man 11
the spectacle 12
the cockfight bust 13
logic 14
the great american motorcycle boots 15
democracy 16
they told me not to sing 18
the malthusian theory 21
beyond the window 22

II
nightmare off bruckner boulevard 25
webster avenue 26
scratch park 27
off southern boulevard 28
the dharma express 29
the bronx vikings 30
jonas 31
gouverneur morris laughs from his grave 32
beyond the crying tenements 34

III
roosevelt's bust 37

IV
saint mary's park
    fuzzy caterpillars 49
    lost playgrounds 52
    the seasons before 54
    rosebud 56
    flesh and blood 57
    the trees of saint mary's 58

V
pastoral esplanades 67
ferry point park 68
the subway grating fisherman 70
maples forever 71
crossing invisible streams 72
saint jude's bazaar 76

*to mary ellen, annemarie, and robert,
and to robert and marguerite—
thank you*

I

the bootblack

the bootblack
neither
creates the shoe
nor kills the cow

has no theories
but the preservation
of leather
and the soul's thin hide

burnishes a small
part of the world
pounding wonder
from the mundane

clodhoppers
loafers
wing tips
combat boots

the legendary
puerto rican fence climbers
pumps and
police brogues

reality is unique
as a world worn foot
these walking streets
are beautiful

my little red fire engine

my little red fire engine
i sit i steer i pedal
toward imaginary disasters
as though i were important
but today no kids are out
to save from the flames
too hot this august morning
for many emergencies
this holy day of obligation
at early mass the stone walls
of saint luke's church
chill the bronx heat
señoras in black dresses
finger rosaries
the last irish knights of columbus
guard lonely pews
priestly latin drifts
through the morning peace
firemen beside the holy water
on the threshold are ready
to scramble but the alarm
does not ring
the offertory bells
startle all to salvation
hook and ladder 29
just across the street
its art nouveau facade
wondrous to a young boy
searching for heroes
and glory
engines shiny
freshblood red behind
a trinity of corniced arches
prepared to rescue all
from mortal infernos

nothing burns
devotional candles melt with prayer
the priest's homily
is in the vernacular
heaven is heaven and hell is hell
earth is the mystery to me
o for the paradise years
before riots and assassinations
and the arson that burns
through the safety of sleep
brickbats bottles the rage of the mob
greet the saviors
so many willing to throw stones
at so few
before despair there is hope
which flickers away
save the apartments we desperately need
the building beside the church
is torched one winter night
the top two floors lost
before the ladder is raised
five stories overhead the lone fireman
directs the hose
he is a silver angel
in the white spotlight
the orange flames
the black sky
the brown smoke
it is all just another insurance payout
a cheap eviction of unwanted tenants
this is the incense
of the church of the bronx
charred tenement skeletons
stand like sentinels of death
acres of crumbled brick and broken glass

fill for years with garbage
weeds grow amidst the rot
faint promise of a green life
the trash is set ablaze
these are the prairies of the slums
where wild dogs scavenge
and there is wailing
and gnashing of teeth
we make our offerings
and we eat the divine
we are blessed and are sent
into the stark sunlight
of bronx streets
at the bakery the cinnamon buns
are still warm
mother perks the coffee
and sends me out to play
in my shiny red
little fire engine
and i roar up and down
but the arsonists are sleeping
and there is no one to save

sledgehammer man

i need a couple bucks he says
sleeveless white tee shirt
skinny muscles
that sledgehammer props him up
that sledgehammer says maybe he'll bust up the place
his friend smiling like something nice gonna happen
he's scowling
i need a couple bucks
and i don't know what to say
i just see that sledgehammer
i need a couple bucks
and uncle reaching towards the cash register for his billy club
i need a couple bucks
and cousin whips a lead pipe
from beside the radiator and says
you're not getting any money
you're not getting any money
and they walk away
the smiler the scowler the sledgehammer
fade in the long streets
to lives of anonymity
because everyone knows al's shanty
gives the best shoeshine in the bronx
but nobody's heard of the sledgehammer robber
nor his smiling sidekick
but maybe if he had said please
maybe
if it weren't for that sledgehammer
he might have gotten some money
free money just for being down and out and telling
some tale of rotten luck but he didn't
maybe he should have tried the pawnbroker
it was a decent sledgehammer
really
quite formidable

the spectacle

they came to see us bleed
we fought like friends
i was bigger and he stronger
so many people gathered one summer sunday afternoon
to watch two kids fight
and blur eyed i saw a man
offer him a toy pistol to beat in my brains with
but he didn't take it
he was above them
a hundred bored people
and we became an event
i could've been watching from my own window
like the great cockfight bust or a minor riot
o blessed and peaceful is the vicarious
yes yes we are the subjects of a wordsworthian poem
i'll bet there are even lakes somewhere
beyond the cloud capped tenements
and if we had some money
we might see some beauty in this too
but we'll crawl out of this half blind
and half dead and our consolation
will be to know there are those worse off
like that highland lass reaping and singing
melancholy and plaintive forever
except now poetry doesn't rhyme
and she harvests subminimum wages
while the molds fill with plastic and metal
in a third world toy factory
where no vote counts but the right one
or the left one and no union strikes
so we gather our leeches where we may and sell them
we make bets on children's fights
and stake our bucks on the rooster's razored claws
and we long for our brief childhood perhaps
if it were not so terrible

the cockfight bust

police barricade the entire street
squad cars detective cars a police bus
spectators everywhere
like celebrity seekers at a broadway opening in some old movie
and down the police lined path
prisoners are herded to meatmarket justice
booked and sentenced
to live their lives in anonymous apartments
to fatten and die in the bronx
but judicious wheels turn slowly
it takes a very long restless time
for two patrol wagons to return and reload
return and reload again and again
everyone gets bored amid all the excitement
so cops run round the corner to roundup strays
escaping through canyons of basements
and catch no one to the crowd's delight
while i count seventy eight men and women
with blankets and picnic baskets
children and babies
parading out to our applause
they wave and cheer back in temporary fame
everyone is happy as when the circus comes
to the puerto rico theater if not happier
because we are all on the stage of a great dramatic irony
and know from the corners of our eyes
that just down the street el lobo sweeps
the sidewalk he don't know nothing
he's just the janitor here
but damn those are his best fighters
hauled off in the unmarked car
while the bull in charge stands
proud as the cock of the walk
and tomorrow at dawn roosters again will crow
will they betray him he wonders
and who got the money

logic

people wonder why i curse so much
and act obnoxious and do everything i can
to keep the blessed human race off my damn back
me who was brought up to be a nice kid
by a nice italian mother and a nice castilian father
taught to speak nicely and to respect others
and elders and all god's creatures and all that crap
like the cat i befriended for ten minutes
and i don't like cats them being sneaky and all
until some stone throwing kids killed it
me who learned in junior high school
while the elders were not watching
or saw only the past or pretended not to notice
when some gang walked into math class
while the teacher was discussing the history of infinity
with academically advanced seventh graders
and beat up a girl who helped grade papers and left
the teacher did not move from his desk
and no counselor came to counsel us
and no principal stopped by to smile and to say
what an unfortunate incident this was and to lie
that this would never happen again it was just
business as usual at arturo toscanini junior high
where gangs chased intellectuals and jews
and anyone else they did not like
and the social studies teacher taught
what a great melting pot america was
when she wasn't at the police station filing assault reports
and with every punch and with every bruise
and with every broken year of my youth i learned
that the more i cursed the less i fought
and the less i fought the less i got beat up
and the less i got beat up the better i looked
in this land of ugliness and that logic of course is power
the power to subdue a curious mind
the power to bully a loving heart

the great american motorcycle boots

black leather
red white and blue paisley inlaid
pointed toes
two american eagles stare me in the face
mean beaked and feisty eyed
all trimmed in neat white stitchery
these are the great american motorcycle boots
and this is the best of all possible ghettos
soon the city will hammer
sheet metal painted with white windows
red and blue curtains
to beautify the abandoned tenements
but the junkies are too stoned to notice
and tourists do not come here
the crazy puerto rican my uncle calls him
just a quiet guy on a loud bike
lean jeans greased hair and a slick jacket
everyone is categorized
johnny the jew who sells shoes on sundays
and slumlords on the side
the dumb guinea bookie
but we ain't hit big yet
the shanty irish cop
who may or may not pay for our honest labor
we shine their shoes with a smile
we hate each other and we love each other
better than we do the government
of this america where only the rich are free
and we are too poor to afford justice
and the loony dude speeds off on his harley
he tips big and his boots beam
bright as an immigrant's smile at the statue of liberty
red blood white eyes blue bruises
the flag won't mean a thing
when the police beat him senseless in the alley

democracy

it was decided by the noisier of the people who are delegated such powers by those who just don't give a damn that america was not such a bad place after all it being july and who needs heat or hot water in this weather anyway and at night when everyone is out the tenements don't look quite so bad and who sees them in the daytime when everyone is sleeping away the heat and the war was good for the economy reducing unemployment by sending the men to war and creating jobs for the women who could work for the guys who did not go to war and who were making big bucks and the underground economy was providing enough luxury items to go round and so it was decided by the noisier of the people who are delegated such powers by those who just don't give a damn that america was not such a bad place after all to celebrate by doing what would have been done anyway as it had become a tradition for the fourth of july so each side sent out its scouts to chinatown and little italy to gather up as much firepower as could be bought or stolen and to smuggle it and stockpile it and to distribute it at just the right time which was sunset on the fourth of july when it was decided by the noisier of the people who are delegated such powers by those who just don't give a damn that america was not such a bad place after all to celebrate by doing what would have been done anyway as it had become a tradition and so the two armies of teenagers too young for draft cards or too mean by means of their criminal records for military service assumed positions on their respective rooftops the ruddy irish above their red bricked tenements and the swarthy puerto ricans and leftover italians above their brown bricked tenements and it was decided by the noisier of the people who are delegated such powers by those who just don't give a damn that america was not such a bad place after all to celebrate by doing what would have been done anyway as it had become a tradition that the war at home had begun which was signaled by a single rocket's red glare which began the shooting of bottle rockets and m-80s and strings of firecrackers and sizzlers which went on for hour after hour keeping the old ladies and babies awake and driving the dogs crazy they cowered in corners like shellshocked veterans though casualties were light as the street was wide and nothing more than a sputtering rocket ever hit the other side mostly everything landed in the street which was by mutual decision a free fire zone and anyone or anything in it an enemy to both sides and mostly there was no one in it except a few unfortunate passersby unaware of this great fourth of july tradition and a line of parked cars which would be pockmarked by morning when the sidewalks were covered with red white and blue paper and the air reeked of sulfur and it was decided that everyone should cease fire and get some chow and shuteye and rest up for the night when it was decided by the noisier of the people who are delegated such powers by those who just don't give a damn that america was not such a bad place after all to celebrate by doing what would have been done anyway as it had become a tradition and the sun went up and down on the ceasefire and the irish and the puerto ricans and the leftover italian guys and their girls and their mothers and fathers and sisters and brothers got back out on our street to hang out to rock babies to gamble to play loud music to drink to gossip to party and to wait to wait to wait for a job for a baby for a draft notice which had become a tradition in not such a bad place after all

they told me not to sing

they told me not to sing
it was sixth grade and all the little puppets
with the sweet little children voices
in the disney exhibit were singing
it's a small world at the world's fair
where they who were not warring or starving
or working paid to stand hours together
on line to see fire dancers and the wonders
of the future like slick cars and clean
nuclear energy
communist china wasn't there because it wasn't
a country but it had the bomb
at the vatican exhibit the sistine chapel and the pietà
god and man forever reaching
the son of god dead in his mother's arms
and we were taught to sing in a castle of a school
collegiate gothic architecture to be exact
with a raised stone basement and a tall grate
upon a concrete moat to keep out the world
william lloyd garrison elementary
the great abolitionist but we were not free
from american values
learn much work hard for the corporation
pay taxes to support the war
buy records and toy machine guns
public school 31
where the teacher took away my tomtom
because i could not carry a beat
but they let me be a dead indian in the play
because i died well
or maybe they were just being kind
i lost so many fights my uncle called me canvasback
but i didn't cry and they told me not to sing
and there was nothing to sing about
where stray dogs tried to sneak into the cafeteria

for a great society lunch
i was door monitor a demotion from safety patrol
a fat kid beneath the central tower's tudor arches
mom did not want me to cross the street anyway
so they took that white plastic sash and shiny silver badge
and gave me door duty
i once admitted a mangy scrawny mutt too kind
to slam the door on its tail and the lunchroom went nuts
crazier than when some kid ate a gefüllte sandwich
i liked the gefüllte fish eaters
i figured they saved me from a lot of fights
because bullies can't beat everyone up all the time
like we could bomb cambodia but not china
and at recess we played the jets and the sharks
without the singing in the west bronx
and without the suicides
we didn't have to kill ourselves
too many others wanted to
and we lived on television dreams
but we did it the american way
tossed a coin to see which class was the sharks
then the fifth and sixth grades got it on
with fists and belts and sticks
ethnicity did not matter
just violence
and the blacks and the puerto ricans and the jews
fought like an italian gang until the bell
rang and we had to pretend to be nice
to each other and to the teacher
who made us sing but not me
because the hand raisers raised their hands
he's flat they said *we can't sing*
because of him and it was always my fault
the flat songs the lost ball games the war
the kennedy assassination the lost dreams

all my fault and she agreed and said
why don't you mouth the words for a while
and i sat through the dumb songs
like a goldfish mouthing through rainbow colored gravel
and the art teacher removed the bowling alley
from my construction paper dream house
but what did she know about my dreams
commuting to the suburbs
only in xanadu is pleasure art
and i took to the treeless streets
mouthing words for years for life
hoping to remain invisible

the malthusian theory

like every long shot it seemed like a sure shot and his legs were so long his stride so swift his torso so lean his need so great he scooped up the stakes from the 534 east 138th street crapshoot and the race was on four lucky gamblers in pursuit what do the losers care who gets the money but it was their game too and it was once their money and what else was there to do now that the game was over and the beer upset so as he passed 530 east 138th street they took after him too he led by ten yards with eight lucky and unlucky gamblers after him and their friends took notice because what else was going on to take notice of so by 526 east 138th street he was twelve yards ahead and eight gamblers and eight lucky and unlucky but otherwise bored friends were hounding him and by 522 east 138th street sixteen acquaintances of theirs must have thought how can he do that to our acquaintances because they took off too while asking each other what did he do anyway and he was sprinting in fine form with thirty two gamblers friends and lucky or unlucky but no longer bored acquaintances huffing and puffing and shouting and screaming which got everybody's attention so by 518 east 138th street thirty two pedestrians took up jogging after him and at 514 east 138th street he was still about five yards ahead of sixty four gamblers friends acquaintances and lucky or unlucky but very excited pedestrians which got the attention of the official 138th street spectators who watch everything and see nothing and sixty four of the fleetest official spectators joined the mob as our part of 138th street ran out of numbers and he turned the corner while one hundred twenty eight not so fast spectators streamed out of their doorways making that two hundred fifty six gamblers friends acquaintances pedestrians and lucky or unlucky fleet or not so fleet but no longer solemn official spectators rushing onto brook avenue to be joined by two hundred fifty six brook avenue strangers making that five hundred twelve gamblers friends acquaintances pedestrians fleet or not so fleet official spectators and lucky or unlucky brook avenue strangers who were met by five hundred twelve lucky or unlucky nondescripts from the mill brook projects making that one thousand twenty four in the curious crowd only twenty four of whom could actually see who got him first or who got the money when the ambulance carried him away which only goes to prove that the hunger of a crowd for entertainment quickly exceeds society's ability to produce amusement

beyond the window

i awaken to the feeling of noise
open the window onto the mob
convinced they would get me at last
burn me like frankenstein
lynch me from a fire escape ladder
but i am fifteen and pretty invisible
and insignificant in the grand scheme of things
this is a major operation
police and people everywhere
i can see which is all that matters
and it is always so exciting
the world beyond the window
but at night in my dreams
i am the sufferers i behold
and it is always so dark
and i am always alone in the unknown
which i know so well
familiar faces chase me
through the familiar streets of childhood
i become a stranger in my own neighborhood
who cannot see his enemy
and awaken in lonely sweat
red lights circling the ceiling
everyone is running or watching
whatever happens i will not be a part
beautiful and ugly are the beholder's eyes
o how do i walk in such a crowded world
in a riot of reality without getting lost

II

nightmare off bruckner boulevard

phantom submarines long to roam
all seven seas but cannot pass
barnacled barges rusting in the channel
of waterlogged nostalgia
for the peaceful streets of wartime
unlocked doors and blackened windows
full employment and boogie woogie
their midnight crews marooned in brown water
beyond cattails and the psychiatric hospital
and the cemetery where tides
sucked coffins from their graves
so these sailors of night
roam with the rowdy street regulars
and the ghostly memories of our parents
while the moon howls at trainloads
of dreamers dragged to destiny
and the deaf school listens to the headlight highway
that crosses avenues without looking
o the horror the horror haunting the dark
where everyplace is a strange neighborhood
drowning these swimmers of shadows
and where are the cameras to tell their tales
those who search for love in the night
why are not they immortal
whose life is an everyday occurrence
these lost navigators adrift upon
the fantastic sidewalks of the landlocked bronx

webster avenue

police prowl
looking for trouble
and coffee
the pub smells warm
of hops and hormones
of wishes realized in jukebox songs
war movies bogart televised sports
all behind those friendly doors
just across the street
and beyond the sinister shadows
of the third avenue el god rest its soul
the evil one makes smiling small talk
with strangers in the night
and off the passenger bridge
from knowledge to intoxication
over the valley of meaningless journeys
onto the sidewalk where many feet have traveled
the forlorn leaps
to a headache and stumbles
for pizza the desperate flesh
afraid and hungry the soul
lonely and thirsting
the self proclaimed retired underwater demolitions expert
is tired of the abuse he says
waves a garrison belt in our faces
does not know who we are and does not care
wants to hurt others before they hurt him
so we give him a beer
let him beat us at midnight checkers
blare the music and a young woman dances
him back to life then he vanishes
bottle in hand up the avenue of vengeance
and unseen in the night
two lovers who do not know it
throw rings of woe to the wind
and grow old together

scratch park

between the future mass murderer
and the extinct tavern
a scratch of asphalt trees
benches beside railroad tracks
that station empty and the train
from here to there seldom stops
concrete chessboards where old men battle
by day by night
beer cans are pawns on checkered squares
the nobility our empty bottles
we drink in history
and drink away our dreams
waiting for dawn
and youth to pass
each tells the other
how the other has erred
and we remain friends
for a forgotten while
and lose ourselves
in what we thought would be fulfillment
empty as that silly solemn darkness
of a warm night when anything may happen
and never seems to at the time

off southern boulevard

off southern boulevard where i will not tell
we find a real dirt tire rutted road
water gullies and pebbles and trees
and we who roam the night are compelled
to subliminal quests for minor satisfaction
so we walk this country lane
because it may not exist in such a city
as this and it curves beyond the known world
not a house in sight such wilderness
surrounds us with ourselves
we step softly in darkness
the breeze blows through our bodies
suddenly trees disappear
beneath our feet is the fine rooftop gravel
of an unknown building and we overlook
the valley where graffitied subway cars sleep
we do not speak so as not to wake them and beyond
tenement eyes stare like stars each light
a distant life on the skyline but we are visible
only to ourselves and we look and look
into the darkness until we leave
to wander and to weary of the night

the dharma express

you never step into the same subway twice
everything changes but the human condition
drop your token or jump your turnstile
hop the dharma express
leave randomly if you will before the last
stop that finality which is always there
waiting for you or for someone else
it matters not so the motorman drives on
and in the end he begins again
thus the last becomes the first
and in the middle huddle
passengers in windowed boxcars
peering over the rooftops of history
or shunning the reflections of darkened windows
while the conductor indifferently
opens and closes her doors for all or for none
and the iron serpent chases its tail
snake eyes in time's great crapshoot
staring down the tunnels of night
and every gambler is surely
the master of his and of her fate

the bronx vikings

i see serpent ships
fierce eyed and grimacing prows
pregnant sails red as villages ablaze
blood and the setting sun red
a favorable wind and sturdy oarsmen
into the sunset which is our east
following the green coast
from the wasteland to warm winters
women and cattle aboard
immigrant explorers beyond the known world
hope the tidal lake karlsefni names it
i see water as blue
as never again
timber and ecstatic grapes
the bountiful beautiful land
salt marshes aswarm with birds
valleys and bluffs rolling to shore
huts are built fish caught
indians trade pelts for string and milk
more pelts less string
then a squabble and stone and iron clash
freydis bares herself
slaps a sword to her breast
like a berserk goddess and the battle halts

the terror of europe retreats to the waves
leaving an ax and runes for the dead
sailing to cold riches lest history repeat
and the warriors celebrate
beneath the bronx sky by the ominous sea

jonas

beyond the ocean
up the crooked strait
past hell gate
and little hell gate
and the kill
where the mainland of hill and marsh
butts the swirling tides
seven miles from civilization
and the muskets of new amsterdam
you buy land from sachem
and rent to sharecropper
so you have come mister bronck
to make a home
on the edge of the chaos of nature
where streams wind through uncleared wilderness
emmaus you call it
and there are trials and revelations
and wars
and patriotic native americans
burn farmhouses to the green green ground
and the land named after the river
that bears your name spits you out
and the land passes away
to morris and his heirs
o you should see what is left of their tombstones
fading in saint ann's churchyard
in a valley of charred bronx tenements

gouverneur morris laughs from his grave

I

gouverneur morris laughs from his grave
sunday congas are distant incessant thunder
enchanted streets swarm and scream
beyond the spikes which ban our flesh
the soul roams at will and the dead man roars
as when he rode reinless horses through revolutionary streets
carriage crash and wooden limb
lame armed and one legged
did the ladies love his bones to death
while he laughed

II

up the once cypressed ridge to grandmother's i go
where the past is always present
musk of soup wisp of ghost
the last trees lean like pale gravestones
in a land where fruit once grew
a harvest of hopeful tenants
to sweat to freeze in aging apartments
to walk through each other's railroad flat lives
the manorial house is another boxcar siding
subways tickle restless coffins

III

all is divine wisdom
what friendly consolation
leglessness so profusely argued
o to part with the other the amputee teased
and his son parted the manor
call the harlem the jordan he quipped

thus mott purchased his haven and the foundry fumed
in the shadows of saint ann's church morris lingers
in the promised land
where tenements rise to burn and crumble

IV

to have traveled so far
to have loved so many
to be buried in the bronx
a landmark in a lost paradise
continental congress and reign of terror
caustic wit and a taste for pleasure
the churchyard cannon has disappeared
did they steal that too
children run from the past
sticks rattle the cemetery fence

V

we too are lovers from ancient families
which prosper and impoverish and wander
celestial plan or random rambling we survive
when death loosens our limbs what land will we haunt
we who rejoice and rebel and enjoy what we may
what sardonic spirit beneath the pavement sprouts
saplings through the rubble of razed streets
grandfather's corpse grinned at the priest who said his eulogy
is it life or is it death that is absurd
those drums those drums those hysterical dead skins

beyond the crying tenements

sometimes moments of great beauty
minor memories of lives never lived slip
through venetian blinds to revive
wallpaper flowers in late sun
linoleum fresh as the lawn
of a great manor on a spring evening
such sweet shade before sunset
a hint of long lost dew
the sweat of creation
in this rent controlled apartment which
my ancestors painted and died

i am too young to worry
i have not been born
but float with the spirits
through trees morris planted
an immigrant arboretum
beyond the crying tenements
the avenue has drowned
the brook flows from the valley
where my lost body walks
like the incarnation of a forgotten god
in a land with no name

III

roosevelt's bust

a lean stern eyed sharp nosed
ivory fdr
dim alley window light
never open shade
railroad flat dining room
that green sofa
where nana will die
that sagging armchair
poppop supervising the yankees
black and white on the gray
long head short body
worn tube television
the table sturdy as
his smiling deathbed spirit
that maddens the priest
my cardboard circus
the crocheted lace tablecloth
sunday funnies and cereal box cutouts
my world is flat but very colorful
orphan annie and dondi
always survive

simmering spices waft
from grandmother's kitchen
she smokes her cigar
she watches the stove
talks to dad alone
incomprehensible castilian
the tin ceiling yellow as chicken skin
soup slowly cooking
an aroma so divine
even statues hunger
mom roots and razzes
bronx cheers
italian damnations

spanish rhythms
grandfather's laughter
such intonations of love
and baseball are universal
only god and government
and grandma's recipe
for wonder remain
eternal mysteries

grand and great
grandchildren live in their photographs
the yanks win and lose
mantle's knees bandaged
his bat healthy
the enameled pig smiles
a ceramic bellyful of thimbles
saved string and tomato pincushions
sideboard drawers of needlepoint and thread
arthritis stopped her stitchery
before i could remember
my elephants parade
amid clowns and acrobats
my awkward hands
topple ladies from white horses
while roosevelt
in honor atop
the parakeet and flower
embroidered doily
armlessly embraces history
on the knickknack buffet

the windup clock
ticks away the present
amid depression blue ashtrays

what a time it was
before i was born
in the beautiful bronx
pristine tenements
beflowered parks
free glassware at five cent
double feature movies
five cent trolleys
through well swept cobblestones
everything cost the nickel
no one had
neighbors thinned the stew
and shared
all night unlocked doors
at christmas santa left
love and best wishes
nothing to fear but hunger
and fascism

spreading across the old countries
new boots for new soldiers
new slogans new marches new weapons
ancient carnage
busby berkeley musicals
movietone news
austria ethiopia
guernica manchuria
a distant world looms
this nation of immigrants
will row row row
with roosevelt across oceans
of unforeseen future
what rendezvous with destiny
a generation of loyal youth
leave school to seek

honest work honest pay
cardboard fills the holes
in weary shoes which do not fit
poor feet are callused and crooked
our fathers' toes never unfurl

the full belly
is the american dream
hoovervilles
the legacy of greed
no feast will erase
memories of young hunger
the solemn inability of parents to provide
holiday lights seem distant as stars
one treeless christmas
father smashes saint nick
reindeer crumble
beneath the angry hammer
plaster dust paint chips childhood
beaten into the tablecloth
his lone protest in a lifetime of labor
tears are reserved
for the suffering of others
lindbergh's baby
the hindenburg disaster
the iron man of baseball
retires and new york grieves

gehrig's speech replays
cameras microphones
ashen faces
free dish theaters and free lunch bars
in the land of the free
in brook avenue back rooms
the bund meets

catholics jews wobblies
the roosevelts are suspect
unions rally in union square
police tail suspicious agitators
social justice may be blasphemy
against the economic pyramid
cops crack loiterers
nightsticks in broad daylight
free beer free apples free shoeshines
for the officer on the beat
city marshals evict the unfortunate
are not responsible for missing valuables
the fbi keeps files
even on eleanor

these are the good old days
so fondly remembered
strikeouts forgotten
home runs sail forever
into happy bleachers
prohibition prohibited
dutch schultz dead
all that beer and no money for drink
this nation thirsts for work
the cigar makers guild
extinguished by the economy
grandpa's fingers have nothing to roll
farmless families head to california
jobless men wander through cities
free rent for the first month
the desperate move often
sons return to empty apartments
and angry landlords
friendly neighbors
whisper the new way home
the family endures

gathers together
the radio warm as a hearth
never lost never sold
fireside chats
sound effect serials
yankee slugfests
the young dream the old forget
baseball transcends history
for a while and the crowds cheer
roosevelt rides triumphant through the bronx
the working poor wave to their hero
forever in the old photograph
tidy streets and stores
no gates no graffiti
aunt helen out her window
mother by the doorway
the tenements are the same
only the poverty has changed
all are immigrants and the immigrants are
fellow americans
compassion is nourished by despair

the war feeds those it does not destroy
pearl harbor bombs the consciousness
blue and gold stars hang in tenement windows
the bronx is a small part
of the great arsenal of democracy
defense contracts war bonds
ration books scrap metal drives
air raid drills in darkened streets
submarines offshore
enemy agents anywhere
loose lips sink ships
the shellshocked do not talk
sons leave sons return

if only in the dreams of mourners
wives work and wait and worry
my grandparents settle
in a railroad flat for the rest of their lives
freedom from want freedom from excess
social security working sons military paychecks
rent paid and food in the pot
the buffet fills with meager memorabilia

grandma's soup remembers
meals that could not be
eight hours eighty years to cook
potatoes gold with spice
chicken melting in broth
time melts the flesh
fingers pale and wrinkled rub
my temples when i am ill
her magic fills all emptiness
with patient love
grandpa is a quiet man
a smile holding a pipe
my circus is a gift
cereal coupons she carefully saved
he watches whitey ford
laughs at clowns between innings
i am the portly ringmaster
tigers are hungry lions roar
loud as times square on victory day
the poor and lousy umpires
are always among us

roosevelt's bust commemorates
the promise of america
the hero who does not survive

the great war he wins
korea vietnam the gimcrackery grows
the beginnings of wars never end
eliot ness chases criminals on late evening reruns
hoover hunts pacifists
spies upon kennedy and king
the invincible heroes are long dead
modern heroes are slain
in slow motion nightly news replays
we are empty of tears
roger maris is no bambino
mother knows the future
is never as good as the past
never again will i taste such soup
the future is death
the past a golden dream
pain digested fun remembered
in words in wonder in silent vision

and in dreams when i wander
through the shadows of that apartment
for one more hug one more smile
one more succulent mouthful
of youth of love
never again will i feel so safe
so afraid of those eyes staring through history
watchful as an eagle
i am what i never could imagine
i have seen america forsake the forgotten
feed the rich starve the poor
people die people die
but no man may abolish memory
no hellfire may kill
human consciousness
the blue ashtrays sit

in mother's kitchen
i have grown i have gone
the embroidery will be given
to my children when i die
and the words i forge with mortal hands

nana held my hand
so tightly her fingers seemed young
she lay on the avocado herringbone couch
rolled over and died the next day
poppop months later in lincoln hospital
rolling his eyes while priest
and pentecostal vied for his soul
the priest fed his ears
the pentecostal filled his belly
in hungry times
death won and he smiled
the yankees lost but we did not care
closets of yellowed magazines
cupboards of dishes but no one was hungry
knickknacks and photographs
lifetimes of possessions scattered and gone
my circus lost in the tears of adolescence
in my grandparents' apartment
amid cheers and feasts
and the fragrance of nostalgia
roosevelt's lost bust stares like remembered love

IV

saint mary's park

fuzzy caterpillars

don't play with fuzzy caterpillars
warns the old woman
black hat black dress
wrinkled cheeks drooping brow
she does not sweat
in the summer sun
she knits
she looks us in the eye
never misses a stitch
never misses an eye
she sits
at the entrance to everywhere
the tenement stoop
the grocery
the park
huddled on a bench
the promenade beneath the flag
where once flowers grew
you'll get pimples
you play with fuzzy caterpillars
we nod politely
she says nothing more
our mothers say hello
and that is all
she smiles
and that is all
we laugh inside
three cousins young with summer
she smiles she knows
we don't give a damn about pimples
or old women
this is america

not the old country
we are three cousins young with summer
what does anyone older than ten
know about anything
we play on fields worn
by scrimmage and baseball
rocks erode with the climbing
we gather catalpa pods
in sacrificial piles
tear them and scatter the seeds
which will not grow for the mowing
we chase each other through wooded paths
reenacting television manhunts
and play with the fuzzy caterpillars
walking them on sticks and fingers
saint mary's park
is a world beyond the immediate
we are immortal
for a while
beyond maroon bricked buildings
with treeless courtyards
and streets amuck with screaming youth
here there are no consequences
to actions
we do not reap what we sow
heroes and villains reincarnate
teams win forever
to invisible cheers
glory and great parks
are fruits of the imagination
there is nothing to fear
but dinner time
on the third day we awaken
to pimples
red bellies pink thighs

which fade quicker than memory
even our mothers are surprised
butterflies scare us more than bees
was it the fuzz
or the caterpillar
or a moth's lesson
we wonder
but not for long
we take stones
and destroy anthills
you'll make it rain
if you kill ants
mother warns
but we know that mud
drives night crawlers from their holes
and what are worms but catalpa pods
with wiggle and blood
slime sometimes
but no fuzz
the sun is a rash
in the graying sky
the old woman knits
the needles crackle
like lightning
at the entrance
to thunder

lost playgrounds

the small playground is nearly empty
our mothers worry as they chat
the longtime sisters
remember moonlight dances
the band in the gazebo
twilight softball games
on diamonds where now gamblers play
fenced gardens
no walking on the grass
irish police with billy clubs
protecting flowers from italians
the rules are quite lax now
at night the park is a wilderness
more frightening than dreams
solitude is unsafe as a mob
we are herded to the main playground
a frenzy of children
shriek in the sprinkler
sing on swings
bicker on see saws
hoot on monkey bars
in the courts beyond
retired italians play boccie
we are lost in play
our mothers lost in gossip
the boccie players lost
in memories of the old days
the polish lady
lost in her knitting
the caterpillars
lost in metamorphosis
the catalpa seeds lost
in america's machinery
somewhere our fathers
are lost in work

they are quiet men
who have forgotten how to scream
lost to them
the summer afternoons
they sweat to give us
the hot sun
the cool water
the rainbow sensations
of young flesh
the growing hunger
we do not yet realize

the seasons before

the fall sun is low
the shadows long
late sunday afternoon
the churches are closed
nana's soup
waits in the pot
i walk with my father
flat feet
trench coat
brimmed hat
like a television detective
a stereotype
he never denied
not bad for a bank clerk
the wind blows
through reddening maples
the seasons before computers
replace brains
and drugsters chase
the last kids from the park
before semiautomatic teens
prowl the hopelessness that is america
four youths wielding
broomsticks and a bowling pin
emerge from the sunset
i am too young to be afraid
and dad too old
that's a nice bowling pin
i say to no one
that's a nice bowling pin
dad says to the big one
the kid hands it to him
they run off into the twilight
red and white and scratched
i set it as the centerpiece

of grandma's table
luscious as her stew
it remains in my room
my favorite trophy
of the long ago time when
we are father and son together
on a field in the bronx highlands
strong and cool as
the autumn wind
the seasons before i learn
we are not immortal

rosebud

down dead man's hill
on a washing machine cover
white enamel
white snow
slick as
white lightning
i lose my mind
in december air
or is it my body
i feel light
as a snowflake
tiny and distant as stars
dad waits
at the bottom of the hill
no i cannot keep
the sleek square
this white rosebud
must remain a gift
to some humble child
who has not planned
on ecstasy
and speeds down the ridge
like a meteor
to land in the bronx
and rise again
the spontaneity of fun
amid the desperate tenements
father waits patiently
i brush snow
off sunday pants
we had not expected
this wandering
we walk home
in quiet darkness
together in the cold

flesh and blood

we climb the approach to janes' hill
his mansion lost
the foundry forgotten
how wondrous to live among the trees
to cast iron for the world
the capitol dome
the savannah fountain
to sell dragons and lions to china
and live unafraid above mott's haven
when parks were unnecessary
the slope is a cowboy movie mountain
i never knew
my father could climb rocks
never knew
i could climb anything
i follow his fingers
holding narrow crevices
too amazed to be afraid
he does all this
wearing a sports jacket and dress shoes
there is no work today
he must have been some kid
heroes never brag about the past
don't say much about the present
at the top we stand like warriors
waiting for a dream vision
the sky is blue beyond
the clouds which roll to the eastern sea
my father is a man of flesh and blood
a modest life a modest death
the bronx grass growing green
over fields and graves
he is the man who made me
the man who gives me life

the trees of saint mary's

buildings die and factories leave
the neighborhood moves
to yonkers or jersey
new neighborhoods arrive
move in move on
across seas and streets
humans flit to certain futures
bronx boulevards lead
to mainland usa
farms platted and wilderness farmed
history is an unremembered
flowerless cemetery
the present is suburban sitcom
its poverty subliminal
this park is the lingering wealth
of an ancient earth
even street signs are mortal
discarded is the decorum
of enamel letters in curved frames
lost the love of here
the elegance of street and avenue
historic names on reflective rectangles
are vestiges of the forgotten
lost are the tales of those who came before
dead the carvers of roads through the wilderness
dead the weckquasgeeks the siwanoy
their long houses long buried
saint ann's churchyard
the last remains of morris manor
the subway station's tile initials
a mere hint of mott haven
art nouveau street lamps
ornate traffic signals
vanished with the cobblestones
mercury lamps glow

like sullen moons
lightpoles are the bare and modern
blighted forests of urban childhood
the past is lost
the future is sold
the trees of saint mary's
are sad as mothers
who have lost their sons
i too will grow away
the trees have roots
sturdier than housing projects
older than tenements
their limbs are prayers on the wind
there is comfort in
those open arms

fires and evictions
redevelopment and decay
seasons of brick and rubble
mother raises me
in the apartment where her parents died
these are the sturdy limbed trees
she knew as a child
she shares them with me
we sit on a bench
of concrete and wood
carvings of long ago romance
submerged in paint
amid splinters
of new love
here retirees rest from long labor
beside shopping bags
of wool and pigeon feed

and bottle babies gurgle
from rocking strollers
breastfeeding has vanished
in the civil rights era
this year's leaves
are green with july
the sky hot with noon
the main concourse
of saint mary's park
on the cypress ridge
in the shade
the same sun
the same trees
the same shade
she walked as a girl with her father

he loved to walk
she loves to walk
i love the trees
the depth of their darkness in the light
i love to walk
through the bronx as she knew it
the ice cream cart
has jingle bells
is christmas in summer
to young mouths
she buys me
what she could not have
when she sunday strolled
through the great depression
with her father
his youngest hope
his little charmer

there were puppet shows
and outdoor movies
no sound
but birds and crickets
the bond of child
and parent never forgotten
the thrill of evening breeze
on the rocks of dead man's hill
they sat together
the wonders of america
flickered before innocent eyes
cowboys villains cops crooks
heroes got their men
ladies kissed their heroes
america seemed orderly
as the circling stars
cobblestones glowed like broadway
and on the walk home
the apartment lights
sparkled with hope
there will be work
there will be food
immigrant streets safe
as the old country
the apartment is crowded with sleep
imagine what shadows
the trees cast in moonlight

i am her only child
in a changing world
she cannot give me
the freedom of her childhood
there are no trolley tracks

to follow to the palisades
no fish in the polluted waters
children who wander
may never return
this is the age
of guns and butter
the rich have the butter
the poor have the guns
death in the jungles
death on the streets
in the age of prosperity
hope erupts to despair
beyond the reach of our hands
the squirrel eats peanuts
his wariness is rhythmic
two bites and a glance
two bites and a glance
presidents and ministers
are not safe in america
two glances and on to the next nut
there are nuts everywhere
mother says
but here the sky is blue and the shade is cool
the benches are lined with drowsy mothers
old women knit winter sweaters
old men throw seed to the birds
they smile like benevolent kings
throwing coin to peasants
startled by a toddler's enthusiasm
the squirrel scurries for the safety of the trees

time stops sometimes on summer afternoons
conversation blurs in the heat

distant as the whine of cicada
the rustle of breeze
and through the invisible doorway we emerge
beyond history and abstraction
to the body and blood
we are
parent and child
forever connected
forever safe
in this womb of trees
floating in a surf of sky
a baby cries and we
are ourselves
who is this woman
who loves me
who will not let me out of her sight
until the waves of seasons
push me into the world
what does she think
pushing me ceaselessly on swings
does she wonder when
i will fly away
does she walk
again through her youth
roaming the bronx with her brothers
does she stroll arm in arm
with father through their long courtship
or simply contemplate dinner
this is the first playground
of the bronx its asphalt skin
is cracked and gray
children are busy
with childhood
there is nothing but this moment
of fun

here the poor forget hunger
here the meek are not afraid
here the sad are lost in laughter
the innocent times before gangs
graffiti the rocks
before the sun is malignant
and the moon a mere golf course
there is nothing but
the exhilaration of life
gravity cannot hold us
we are seeds on the wind
sent forth from timeless trees
the falling from youth
seems eternal
the flight of maple wings
the plunge of acorn and pod
we land in the green world of infinite summer
the trees will not grow old
the trees will keep us forever safe
in the shade of knowledge and life
saint mary's park is heaven on earth
hell is the streets where we suffer and die

V

pastoral esplanades

pastoral esplanades were the streets where we played
o the hills o the dales o happily
bleating we lamb gamboled
the concrete pastures of the beautiful bronx

woolly wild we ran and feared no fate
frenzied frivolous too young to be damned
though pedestrians panicked and cursed
death's shepherd would not fleece us

and glorious the metermen jingled and glorious the metermaids sang
in metered bush beneath steel bough of streetlight
echoing with sylvan joy the festive tenements
where dionysian oracles staggered and moaned

o did shopping bag ladies murmur melancholy strains
o were fire escapes ancient pathways to olympus
over the lofty rooftops jets droned like warring titans
and promethean tears rained upon the caucasian skyline

in the lush of this asphalt arcady did we leap
amuck with wonder and joy at the lovely world
we will never grow old we will never grow weary
of sailing the winds of summer never

behold the triborough bridge sleeping
like cerberus across the hell gate

ferry point park

we may turn our backs
on housing project and cemetery
pretend to see the ocean
beyond gulls cawing over the sound
really the restless east river
which ebbs and flows whirling with tides
from sunrise to hell gate
but the horizon is the whitestone bridge
a turquoise arch suspended overhead
vibrant with hum of car and truck and seabound wind
there are no white stones
no ferries
dad and i fished here once
no fish
just empty fields and a busy bridge
and waves to tangle bait amid the boulders
that prop up a land of landfills
and buttress the buttresses of a long road
which crosses even the sky
to the green suburban shores
of queens beyond unswimmable waters
and westchester creek
its half sunk rusted barge
aglow and unmoving in the bronx sun
temporarily triumphant
in its long war with eternity
while we forget the lives which keep us apart
and stand together father and son
new york's skyline lost in the southwest haze
strangely alone and strangely united
in the awkward peace which blows
just beyond our daily world
with nothing to say and no need to speak
on the shore of the land of our birth
beyond a sea of ancestors

one to die here one to leave
but we do not think of the future
and a narrow strip of beach amid the rocks
where footprints wash away
and that bridge
with the promise of there being someplace to go
and the clouds
and a sky towering over the towers
with the promise of heaven

the subway grating fisherman

i am a subway grating fisherman
everything i can imagine is down there
slightly below the sidewalk
in subterranean gills
slightly out of reach
beneath steel waves
on the cement shores of the abyss
of eternal boredom
such is youth
a stringed magnet
the glisten of hope in the sludge
to be caught by a patient hand
and desperate faith in the renewal
of the familiar
let the big boys fish
with hot bubble gum or cold vaseline
for what coin falls from the rich
i haul in the bottle caps
which no one wants
so beautifully
ordinary

maples forever

i hope the maples are still there
and the wading pool and monkey bars
the little playground off brook avenue
leafy maples that hide alleys and backyards
the gray windows of sweaty kitchens
curtained bedrooms for the weary to rest
and shade the sandbox and the sidewalk checkerboard
thirteen squares the center is dead man's land
we shoot bottle caps from number to number
a game of skully beneath rustling leaves

beyond the branches are schools
that teach how not to be young
industry feeds educated workers
the american dream not dreaming artists
what we draw in chalk will wash away
fantasies fade in the fluorescence of technology
money is real the sky but a blue
emptiness of untouchable clouds
and a drizzle of maple pods spiraling down
slow and steady and fruitless upon the asphalt

future forests blowing away
like the wonders of childhood

crossing invisible streams

school teaches all a nuclear man must know
montgomery
vietnam
purple mountains
bloody plains
but this land is mystery
submerged in sidewalk
the forgotten earth
the stream of smooth stones
mosholu mosholu
it babbles off the tongue
mosholu mosholu
stream of smooth stones
native americans named it
and vanished like the water
street signs mock the history beneath our feet
hills hidden by tenements
invisible streams trapped in sewers
mortar and brick
cement and stone
the landscape is a mutation of the inanimate
mosholu parkway the reality we know so well
parkway parkway
mowed grass embanks the asphalt
the tarmac is a free fire zone
where they wait to break our bones
they who are not at war overseas
ready to run their cars over our sneakers
to shove us with their bumpers
just for laughs
they will catch reruns of lucy
before the nightly news
they have color televisions
better to see the blood with
jungle blood street blood

black and white and yellow
the blood is red
redder than lucy's hair
the real world is bloodier
than john wayne movies
we gather to charge
like hollywood indians we yell
but we do not cry
we will survive
eight thousand boys
dewitt clinton high school's
wary students learning america
the largest boys' school short of the army
there are no green lights
no negotiations
no plans but instinct
this is the war of generations
and we have come to do battle
where the lost stream runs
invisible as innocence
it begins with a few bold scouts
a spearhead of impromptu volunteers
then we swarm the cars
no one says let's go
we just do
a battalion of boys who simply want to go home
dodging impatient commuters
grandmothers in mustangs who seek revenge
on wayward youth
housewives out for a few thrills
businessmen too busy to join the war
o how they love the action
but they can't bash all of us all the time
we will survive
we ford the highway

the city lies ahead
safety is in the herd and we stampede the trail
through mosholu park
a few trees mowed grass an old name
benches where veterans
play chess and handicap horses
here traitors ambush us
a barrage of stones and pennies
we are many and desperate
they are few and they flee
we overrun the wall
up the ancient el station's stairs
to fall is perilous
our feet are young
we hurl our momentum
at gates and turnstiles
surly cops with clubs and guns
check subway passes
cull those to search
for weapons and draft cards
most of us are deemed
only old enough for football
the army may want us someday
but the conductor does not
he closes electronic doors on our mortal necks
while our buddies help us aboard
all we have is each other
we pack into the train
restless and weary and rowdy as soldiers on leave
deploying to tenements and projects
warm girl friends and minimum wage jobs
the rails cross the bronx skyline
steel stanchions rooted
in the stream that became jerome avenue
the woodlawn train begins at the cemetery

and disappears into the ground
woodlawn woodlawn
trees and tombstones on the lawns of death
war memorials remember the fallen
do the dead learn
the secrets of the land beneath the asphalt
do they wander
the lost paradise of the bronx
there will be new wars
there will be new warriors
the tunnel leads to wall street
the heart of america
like our parents we are
ceaseless commuters
carried by unrelenting wheels
we too love the dauntless lucy
and admire the streamlined cars
that race through the commercials
which fund the nightly news
where officers of the peace
beat peaceful demonstrators
and the war continues to bring peace to vietnam
police bleed
protesters bleed
soldiers bleed
civilians bleed
but most endure
we watch the blood
we await our futures
alone in hopeful fear
we are young warriors wandering
the asphalt concrete wilderness
we are young warriors crossing
invisible streams to survive

saint jude's bazaar

money comes and goes but gimcrackery is forever
we toss coins on lucky numbers
we are nickel and dime gamblers
on the great wheel of fortune
hopelessly lost in ordinary lives
in toil and worry
in the ebb and flow of currency
summers of sweat
cold tenement winters
days of work nights of dreams
life must be better
in the suburbs we watch on television
the suburbs which are always
just beyond the next river
we have crossed the harlem
but we have not been transformed
we seek the impossible but savor trifles
we have passed through the darkness
into a place of noise and light
the church is empty
the basement smells of sawdust and beer
it's las vegas night the local parishioners
pray to beat the house
they win they lose they cycle
through various heavens and hells and emerge
happy to be on earth
only mildly hung over
only moderately broke
they join us in the playground carnival
here pocket change can become
tangible trophies of good fortune
here the game tents are full
of plastic toys of plaster lamps
radios ashtrays stuffed animals
pen knives and cigarette lighters

and the wheels spin
and the wheels spin
the ferris wheel turns and turns
cotton candy winds out of sticky machines
people walk round and round
shedding money as they go
summer is spinning away
autumn nights are long and cool
that geisha lamp will brighten them
that stuffed bear will bring warmth
when the furnace is broken when the super is drunk
when the landlord did not pay the fuel bill and there is no heat
and in the midwinter darkness i will see it again
see it as i do each year at the ten o'clock raffle
a heavenly vision over upturned faces
the crowd silent the ferris wheel still
passengers swaying in the starless haze
the tickets are turned in a clear rotisserie
rising and falling and rising again
hope burns in the night
the adults look grim but the children
grasp the impossible
the children whose imaginations are more vivid
than the sticky asphalt crowded
with the odds that are against them
the priest slowly climbs the steps
the priest bares his innocent arm
the priest unlocks the door to eternal childhood
and raises the chosen one to the sky
from above a voice pronounces the numbers
the winner comes forth to fulfill
the dreams of the multitude
white stubs rain down from losing hands
there is nothing to do but return to the bronx
and i will see it again and again

when i am old and my knees are bad and my hair is falling out
the big red bicycle
a made in america schwinn
hand brakes
gears to shift
on this i will ride
through an imaginary childhood
down tree lined streets
neighbors will smile and wave
i will have friends and we
will fish and play baseball
in little league teams with uniforms
and ride our bicycles home for lunch
and year after year we make the pilgrimage
to saint jude's bazaar
and the big red bicycle raffle
one dollar a ticket but i never win
and year by year i realize
how foolish it would be
to ride this bicycle through the bronx
dodging trucks and bicycle bandits
and i have no friends to protect me
father wins a car
uncle hits the number and buys a mustang
but we never leave the bronx
we always return to the treeless streets
the tenement has not been incinerated
the apartment has not been burglarized
when we turn on the lights
the roaches make a polite exit
and life is as beautiful
as it would be anywhere
there is food in the refrigerator
there is love at the table
and i have not been killed

defending my big red bicycle from street gangs
in my room the calcium paint has chipped
white craters float like clouds
and the streetlight shines like the moon
at dawn heat rises through the radiators
hot water flows through the pipes
teddy bear has gone
to teddy bear heaven
the exotic lamps are hooked
to automatic timers to fool burglars
i follow the american dream
i work hard buy a house and a rusting chevy
i play the state lottery
the odds look good to a poet
at sunrise i walk to stretch the stiffness from my joints
my number has not come up
and i believe in miracles
they are everywhere
in the hope
in the suffering
in the fluttering emptiness of the suburban morning

www.ingramcontent.com/pod-product-compliance
Lightning Source LLC
Chambersburg PA
CBHW071332190426
43193CB00041B/1752